Photography
Portfolio
2014

Joseph Fleming

Joseph Fleming

Original Fine Art Photographs

Decades of being around accomplished talent producing absolutely phenomenal quality work has taught that we are capable of greatness. It is possible to meet our destiny and become it. Experiencing excellence done with such apparent ease and humble selfless gratification is the motivation for this photography. Most important was having the freedom

Being colorblind gives an advantage when composing black & white... less confusion.
This special collection selected from thousands of captures. All images were framed
in the camera and presented without edits, genuine as seen through the lens.
RAW conversion applied by proprietary panchromatic process.

Limited edition prints available from original source files.

info@ BEACHNOISE.com

0531

0780

0826

1581

1608

2180

2467

2631

2929

3147

3151

3720

4035

4099

1265

4533

5492

5511

5750

5781

5844

6095

6176

7182

7339

7656

7939

8173

8470

8889

9024

9430

www.ingramcontent.com/pod-product-compliance
Lightning Source LLC
Chambersburg PA
CBHW050751180526
45159CB00003B/1419